MEDITATIONS WITH MEISTER ECKHART

Introduction and Versions by
Matthew Fox, o.p.

BEAR & COMPANY
Rochester, Vermont

For all those daring to make the spiritual journey
and to befriend the darkness.
may the hope of Meister Eckhart accompany you
when he says:

> "The path is
> beautiful and pleasant and joyful and
> familiar."

Bear & Company
One Park Street
Rochester, Vermont 05767
www.InnerTraditions.com

ISBN 978-0-939680-04-7

Library of Congress Card Number 82-71451

Printed and bound in the United States

30 29 28 27 26 25 24 23 22

Cover art and line illustrations by Candy Tucci, osf

Introduction

Meister Eckhart (1260-c. 1329) was mystic and prophet, feminist and philosopher, preacher and theologian, administrator and poet, a spiritual genius and a declared heretic. While all reputable scholars today agree he was unjustly condemned—his condemnation bears all the earmarks of an attempt to silence his prophetic preaching on behalf of the poor in his society—his way of spirituality remains too little known in the West. While Hindus and Buddhists claim Eckhart as one of their own, while psychologists like Jung and Marxists like Bloch and Fromm learn from him, many, many Christians hardly know the name, much less the spiritual tradition he represents so beautifully.

That tradition is the creation-centered spiritual tradition. While the fall-redemption tradition begins spirituality with humanity's sinfulness, the creation-centered tradition that Eckhart represents begins with humanity's potential to act divinely both by way of compassion and of beauty-making and sharing. To begin with sin is not Good News—it is not news for nothing is more obvious to observers of human history—especially those of us in the 20th century—than our capacity for sin; and it is not good and does not arouse goodness or the good power of imagination that can create alternatives to the cycles of human folly and sin and violence.

Of the spiritual pathway that Eckhart names, he himself says: "This path is beautiful and pleasant and joyful and familiar." Why does he claim that his way is "familiar"? Is there a haunting recognition of the creation-centered way that conjures up childhood or other periods of truth in our lives? Is it because what is beautiful and pleasant and joyful is necessarily familiar because it is memorable and, try as we might, we do not forget such deep experiences of ecstasy and beauty? Is Eckhart's way a familiar way because it is so non-elitest and because all persons whether women or men, lay or cleric, old or young, poor or comfortable already have taken this

3

journey at some time in their lives? Eckhart was no closet-monk, no spiritual romantic longing for a cloister of refuge from the pain and politics of involvement in society. Highly educated that he was, professor that he was, still his profoundest spiritual maturation occurred not in academia but in mixing with the lay feminist movement of Beguines of his day. Perhaps that is why he could declare, contrary to those who find a comfortable refuge in academia, that "the most noble kind of knowledge is learned by living." The creation spiritual tradition that Eckhart preaches is a tradition that believes that life itself—living and dying, growing and sinning, groaning and celebrating—is the creative energy of God, God's *Dabhar*, in motion. Eckhart learned to trust life and his own life experiences. And this he taught others to do as well. As important as knowledge is to our living, still the spiritual way begins with the heart. "Where should we begin? Begin with the heart. For the spring of life arises from the heart and from there it runs in a circular manner" he observes. For Eckhart, to be spiritual is to be awake and alive—the holiness of life itself absolutely fascinated Eckhart—creation itself was for him the primary sacrament and for this reason he informs us that the spiritual life begins where life does: from "the spring of life" or the heart.

The spiritual way that Eckhart invites us to enter into and to journey with him on can be named as a four-fold way.[1] This four-fold way is profoundly different from the three-fold path that the Neo-platonist tradition has preached and which has dominated almost all thought about spirituality in the West for centuries. Eckhart names our spiritual journey in the following fashion:

1. Creation. Our first experience of God is in the beauty and glory, the power and the potential, the unlimits and the brilliance of creation itself. The cosmos and ourselves as microcosms and as images of the Creator are experienced not as objects "out there" but as God-bearing sacraments.

2. Letting Go and Letting Be. As divine as all creation is, the human person must learn to let go of things in order to let things be things and in order that reverence might be learned. Things are not bad

[1]See Matthew Fox, "Meister Eckhart on the Four-Fold Path of a Creation-Centered Spiritual Journey," in Matthew Fox, ed., *Western Spirituality: Historical Roots, Ecumenical Routes* (Santa Fe: Bear & Co., 1981), pp. 215-248. For Meister Eckhart's works in a critical and reliable edition see Matthew Fox, *Breakthrough: Meister Eckhart's Creation Spirituality in New Translation* (Garden City, NY: Doubleday Image, 1980).

4

but the human propensity to cling to things is harmful and creates the dualisms that result in all sin. When we let go and let be we learn new levels of trust including trust in the dark and in our experiences of nothingness, both personal and political.

3. Breakthrough and Birth of Self, God and Self as child of God. Following on the emptying of path two comes union, realization of union and birth. For Eckhart all experience of union is meant to bear fruit—"by their fruit you will know them"—and so creativity is as much a test of true spirituality as it is a result of it.

4. The New Creation: Compassion and Social Justice. The human person can be creative in evil ways—we can use our imaginations to create more pain and violence, more acts of sadism instead of less sadism. Thus Eckhart insists in very strong language that our spiritual life is not ended with creativity but rather we are to employ creativity for the sake of personal and social transformation. And justice and compassion are the tests of this authentic deployment. So important is justice to Eckhart's understanding of the spiritual journey that he can say: "The person who understands what I have to say about justice understands everything I have to say."

But here, with compassion, the spiritual path does not end: Rather, it returns to its beginning, for we were born in compassion since "the first outburst of everything God creates is always compassion." The spiritual journey is a spiral that returns us to our starting point. But our journey is an ever-growing and expanding spiral in which our growth knows no limits.

This four-fold path of Eckhart and of the creation spiritual tradition can be summarized in the following manner:
1. **Via positiva.**
2. **Via negativa.**
3. **Via creativa.**
4. **Via transformativa.**
How does this compare with the much more familiar three-fold path from Neo-platonism? This path is labeled as follows:
1. **Purgation.**
2. **Illumination.**
3. **Union.**
Note first that Path one—the via positiva—is totally lacking in the Neo-platonic schema. The purgation stage does not correspond to the full richness of Eckhart's via negativa, however it does come

under that heading. Both illumination and union would come under Eckhart's via creativa though they represent only part of Eckhart's meaning since this tradition in no way emphasizes the importance of creativity. For example in the all too familiar 750-page volume on "The Spiritual Life: A Treatise on Ascetical and Mystical Theology," the Rev. Adolphe Tanquerry does not even have an entry in his index for "creativity" or "beauty" or "artist" but he does have over four inches of entries on "mortification," "concupiscence," "penance." While five inches of index are accorded the non-biblical category called "contemplation," no entry at all is present under the title "compassion." This, even though Jesus told his followers in Luke's Gospel: "Be you compassionate as your Creator in heaven is compassionate." Thus there is no via transformativa in the three-fold pathway we have inherited from Neo-platonism. With no via positiva the via negativa gets distorted and is easily reduced to asceticism and acts of the will in controlling and putting down human passion. Eckhart has a blunt answer to such spiritual violence when he says "asceticism is of no great importance" and explains why this is so (see page 58). Thus, the Neo-platonic tradition lacks 50% of the life-experiences (via positiva and via transformativa) of the creation-centered tradition; and within the two stages it does elaborate on, the via negativa and via creativa, it lacks another 50% of what the creation tradition develops. This means that the West has been operating on about 25% of human spiritual potential for centuries. Imagine a four cylinder car with only one cylinder working—that is the kind of spiritual energy loss we have been operating on in the West when we have let the three-fold path of the Neoplatonic tradition guide us. No wonder a spiritual energy crisis has come over us in the West and dualisms play a greater role in our lives than do our shared humanity and divinity. No wonder we are in the precarious position as regards human survival and Gospel living that we are!

Clearly it is time for a new beginning; which, in fact, is the far more ancient beginning since the oldest Jewish and Christian Scriptures —those of the Yahwist author in the tenth century before Christ— are creation-centered. And Jesus, along with most other prophets before and after him, was creation-centered. It is time for some Meditations with Meister Eckhart.

Eckhart's pathway and that of the creation tradition that he represents is a simple way. It does not demand a lot of baggage for the journey, it demands no gurus, no fanciful methods other than

6

the discipline that all art requires, no excessive exercises or retreats. This is why Eckhart can call his a "wayless way" that is available to all, and also why he points out that "she who has found this way needs no other." In spiritual matters as in all deep human endeavors, the simple is what lasts, for as Eckhart puts it: "the soul does not grow by addition but by subtraction." After all, what spirituality other than a simple one could possibly lay claim to being a pathway that is "beautiful and joyful, pleasant and familiar"?

The translations and adaptations and arrangements of Eckhart's words in this text are my own. Like any translator who has sat at the feet of a master of profound experience of the divine, I am humbled by this task. Yet I am comforted by Eckhart's own words; "When we speak of divine matters, we have to stammer, because we are forced to express our experiences in words." May Eckhart's and my stammering assist the stammering of the reader. May the reader enjoy these meditations and be deepened and affirmed in them. And may the reader be made more courageous and prophetic by them, so that it may be said of you as of Meister Eckhart, that you were henceforth "unbelievably happy, never overcome by fear and the fearful, and always in trouble." The translations of Eckhart in these pages are my own. At times, perhaps 5% at the most, I have adapted a line here or there for our contemporary use. If the reader would prefer to call these "versions" rather than translations, that is fine with me. Knowing Eckhart as I do, I think he would approve.

**Institute of Creation-Centered
Spirituality
Mundelein College, Chicago, IL**

**October, 1981, the 800th anniversary
of Saint Francis of Assisi's birth**

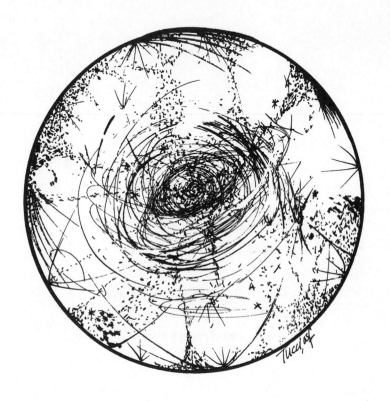

PATH I:

CREATION

(via positiva)

When I dwelt in the ground,
       in the bottom, in the stream, and
       in the source of the Godhead,

No one asked me where I was going or
       what I was doing.

Back in the womb from which I came,
       I had no God
          and merely was myself.

And when I return
     to God and to the core, the soil, the ground,
     the stream and the source of the Godhead,
No one asks me where I am coming from
     or where I have been.

For no one misses me
     in the place
     where God ceases to become.

Now the moment I flowed out from the Creator
    all creatures stood up and shouted:
    "Behold, here is God!"

They were correct.
For you ask me: Who is God? What is God?
I reply: Isness.
Isness is God.

Where there is isness, there God is.
Creation is the giving of isness from God.
And that is why
        God becomes
where any creature expresses God.

Isness is so noble. No creature is so tiny that
it lacks isness.
If a caterpillar falls off a tree,
 it climbs up a wall
   in order to preserve its isness.
 So noble is isness!

If you were able to deprive God of isness,
a stone would be more noble than God, for a
stone has isness.

   What is God?
    God is!

14

Apprehend God in all things,
    for God is in all things.

Every single creature is full of God
    and is a book about God.

Every creature is a word of God.

If I spent enough time with the tiniest creature—
even a caterpillar—
        I would never have to prepare a sermon. So full of God
            is every creature.

Earth cannot escape heaven,
     Flee it by going up,
          or flee it by going down,
    heaven still invades the earth,
       energizes it,
               makes it sacred.

All hiding places reveal God.
If you want to escape God,
     S/he runs into your lap.

For,
     God is at home.
     It is we who have gone out for a walk.

God is a great underground river

that no one can dam up

and no one can stop.

Now God creates all things
    but does not stop creating.

God forever creates
    and forever begins to create
    and creatures are always being created
    and in the process of beginning
    to be created.

Now I shall tell you something I have never
spoken of before.
God enjoys him/herself.
In the same enjoyment in which God enjoys him/herself,
S/he enjoys all creatures.

God
     finds joy and rapture
                      in us.

All that is good in creatures—
    all their honeysweetness-

                    comes from God.

All things are pure and noble in God.

We love everything according to our own goodness.

We are to love all things that lead us to God—

That alone is love.

God's being is my being

and God's primordial being
is my primordial being.

Wherever I am,
there is God.

The eye with which I see God
    is the same eye with which God sees me.

God created all things in such a way
  that they are not outside himself,
  as ignorant people falsely imagine.
Rather,
All creatures flow outward, but nonetheless remain
within God.
God created all things this way:
  not that they might stand outside of
  God, nor alongside God,
  nor beyond God,
but that they might
  come into God
  and receive God
  and dwell in God.
For this reason everything that is
  is bathed in God,
  is enveloped by God,
  who is round-about us all, enveloping us.

Being is God's circle

and in this circle
all creatures exist.

Everything that is in God
is God.

I have often said
that God is creating the entire universe
fully and totally
in this present now.
Everything God created six thousand years ago—and even
            previous to that—as he made the world,
God creates now all at once.

Now consider this: God is in everything, but
God is nowhere as much as he is in the soul.
There,
where time never enters,
where no image shines in,
in the innermost and deepest aspect of the soul
God creates the whole cosmos.

Everything which God created millions of years ago
and everything
     which will be created by God after millions of years—
if the world endures until then—
God is creating all that in the innermost and deepest realms
     of the soul.
Everything of the past
and everything of the present
and everything of the future
God creates
in the innermost realms of the soul.

We ought to understand God equally in all things,
for God is equally in all things.

All beings
          love
                    one another.

All creatures
                    are interdependent.

If I were alone in a desert
   and feeling afraid,
I would want a child to be with me.
For then my fear would disappear
   and I would be made strong.
This is what life in itself can do
because it is so noble, so full of pleasure
   and so powerful.

But if I could not have a child with me
I would like to have at least a living animal
at my side to comfort me.

Therefore,
let those who bring about wonderful things
in their big, dark books
take an animal—perhaps a dog—
to help them.

The life within the animal
will give them strength in turn.
   For equality
gives strength in all things
and at all times.

The seed of God is in us.
    Now
         the seed of a pear tree
           grows into a pear tree;
        and a hazel seed
          grows into a hazel tree;

     a seed of God
       grows into
            God.

God

       loves the soul so deeply
       that were anyone to take away from God
       the divine love of the soul,
that person would kill God.

       If you were to let a horse
          run about in a green meadow,
    the horse would want to pour forth its whole strength
          in leaping about the meadow.
So too
it is a joy to God
               to have poured out
      the divine nature and being
         completely into us

      who are divine images.

This I know.

  That the only way to live

        is like the rose

which lives

        without a why.

You might ask life itself over a period of a thousand years
the following question: 'Why are you alive?' And still the only
response you would receive would be: 'I live so that I may live.'
      Why does this happen?
      Because life rises from its own foundation
      and rises out of itself.
      Therefore,
           life lives without a reason—
           life lives for itself.

What is life?
Life is a kind of boiling over
      in which a thing wells up within itself,
      floods itself and overflows
      pouring itself into all of its parts
until finally
      it spills over
      boiling and overflowing
      into something external as well.

When we say 'God is eternal,' we mean: God is eternally young.
God is
      ever green, ever verdant, ever flowering.
Every action of God
      is new, for he makes all things new.
God is the newest thing there is; the youngest thing there is.
God is
      the beginning
and if we are united to him we become new again.

      *   *   *   *

      My soul is as young as the day it was created.
      Yes, and much younger!
      In fact, I am younger today than I was yesterday,
and if I am not younger tomorrow than I am today,
      I would be ashamed of myself.
People who dwell in God dwell in the eternal now.
There, people can never grow old.
There, everything is present and everything is new.

God is

voluptuous

and

delicious.

*   *   *   *

All creatures

speak of God

the way I have.

If the only prayer

you say in your entire life
is 'Thank You,'

that would suffice.

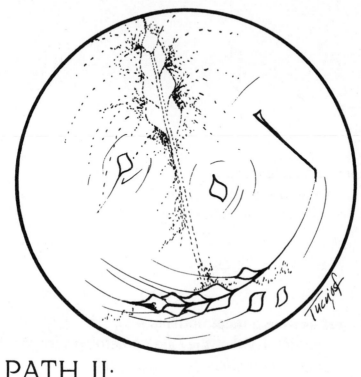

PATH II:

LETTING GO and LETTING BE

(via negativa)

Only God has isness.
>Therefore everything that is created
>>is in itself nothing.

All creatures are a mere nothing.
>I do not say that they are something very slight
>or even something,
>>but that they are a mere nothing.

All creatures
      have been drawn from nothingness
And this is why
their origin is nothingness.

The whole universe
      as compared to God
            is as nothing.

The color of a wall
      depends on the wall.

      In the same manner
the isness of creatures
      depends on the love of God.

Take the color from the wall and the color would cease to be.
      So too,
            all creatures would cease to exist
if they were separated from
            the love that God is.

Outside of God

There is

nothing

but nothing.

All the creatures

        cannot
            express God. For they are not
receptive of what God is.

        God
        the ineffable one
        has no name.

        The divine one
is a negation
        of negations

and
    a denial
        of denials.

God is nothing.
    No thing.
        God is nothingness;
        and yet God is something.

        God is neither this thing nor that thing
        that we can express.
        God is a being beyond all being;
        God is a beingless being.

Truly God
        is a hidden God.

All the names which the soul gives to God,
    it receives from the knowledge of itself.

But the ground of the soul is dark.

The ineffable One has no name.

The naked God
    is without a name
    and is
        the denial of all names
    and has never
        been given a name
    and so remains
    a truly hidden God.

God's darkness
     is a superessential darkness.

     A mystery behind mystery,
     a mystery within mystery that no light
has ever penetrated.

     The final goal of being
     is the darkness and the unknowability of the hidden
     divinity,
     which is that light which shines
          'but the darkness cannot comprehend it.'
                           (Jn.1.5)

     God acts but the Godhead does not act.
The mystery of the darkness of the eternal Godhead is unknown
          and never was known
          and never will be known.

     God dwells therein, unknown to himself/herself.

God is a being beyond being and a
nothingness beyond being.

The most beautiful thing
which a person can say about God
would be for that person to remain silent
from the wisdom of an inner wealth.
So,
be silent
and quit flapping your gums about God.

God is not found in the soul by adding anything,
    but by a process of subtraction.

How should you love God?
I will tell you.
Love God as God is—
this means: Love God as God is
    a not-God,
    a not-mind,
    a not-person,
    a not-image.
More than this, love God as God is
    a pure, clear One
    who is separate from all twoness.

One should love God mindlessly,
by this I mean that your soul ought to be
without mind or mental activities
or images or representations.
Bare your soul of all mind
And stay there without mind.

Moreover, I advise you
        to let your own 'being you' sink away
        and melt into
                God's 'being God.'
        In this way your 'you' and God's 'his,'
                will become a completely one 'my.'
        And you will come to know his changeless existence
                and his nameless nothingness.

Now pay attention.

If the soul wishes to be effective inside itself, it must
gather together all its powers and call them back
from all scattered activities to an internal and
centering activity. Consider this story.

A pagan scholar was dedicated to the science of arithmetic
and concentrated all his powers on it. He was sitting by the
fire one day making calculations when someone came by,
drew his sword, and not knowing who the scholar was,
exclaimed: "Tell me this instant what your name is or I will
kill you!" The scholar was so engrossed in his science that
he neither saw nor heard the soldier. All he needed to do to
save his life was to say: "My name is such and such," but
he was too engrossed to do even that. The enemy screamed
loud and fierce, but he still did not answer and his enemy
cut off his head.

This took place in pursuit of the truth of the natural
sciences. How much more ought we to direct all our powers
of concentration and letting go to that foundation where
our treasure lies hidden.

For the will to be free,
       it needs to let go and return
              to its prime origin.

For the intellect to be free,
       it must become naked and empty and
       by letting go to return to its prime origin.

We become a pure nothing by an unknowing knowledge
which is

       emptiness
       and solitude
       and desert
       and darkness
       and remaining still.

Think of the soul as a vortex or a whirlpool
    and you will understand how we are to
Sink
    eternally
        from negation
            to negation
                into the one.

And how we are to
Sink
    eternally
        from letting go
            to letting go
                into God.

I pray God

to rid me

of God.

The highest and loftiest thing that one can let go of is
to let go of God for the sake of God.

God's exit

is

her entrance.

The more you seek God, the less you will find God.

If you do not seek God,

you will find God.
God does not ask anything else of you
except
that you let yourself go
and let God
be God
in you.

Above all else, then;

Be prepared at all times
        for the gifts of God
        and be ready always
                for new ones.
For God is a thousand times
        more ready to give
                than we are

                        to receive.

As God is omnipotent in his deeds,
        so too the soul is equally profound
                        in its capacity to receive.

There,
>   where clinging to things ends,
>   is where God begins to be.

If a cask is to contain wine,
>   you must first pour out the water.
>   The cask must be bare and empty.

>   Therefore,
if you wish to receive divine joy and God,
>   first pour out your clinging to things.

Everything that is to receive
>   must and ought to be

>   empty.

It is a delusion to think
     that we can obtain more of God
         by contemplation
         or by pious devotions
         or by religious retreats

   than
         by being at the fireplace
         or by working in the stable.

For the person who has learned letting go and letting be
     no creature can any longer hinder.
     Rather,
         each creature points you toward God
         and toward new birth
     and toward seeing the world as God sees it:
     Transparently!

Thus all things become nothing
              but God.
     And we learn
         to know with God's knowledge
         and to live with God's love.

Transformed knowledge,

which is an unknowing,

is the way of transparent knowing,
it is the way
of unselfconsciousness.

When you learn this
you can learn everything
and return to everything
and praise everything.

*   *   *   *

Everything praises God.

Darkness,
            privations,
                        defects,
                                    evil too

praise God and bless God.

"Into the sea all the rivers go, and yet the sea is never filled, and still to their goal the rivers go." (Qo. 1.7)

All creatures flow and return to their source. Transformed knowledge and love draw up and lead and bring the soul back into the first source of the One, the Creator of all in heaven and on earth.

What is created flows out but remains within. So,

when we return to our first origin, which is our primal purity, we discover our freedom and are free.

Asceticism
        is of no great importance.

There is a better way to treat one's passions
       than to pile on oneself ascetic practices
       which so often reveal a great ego
       and create more, instead of less, self-consciousness.
  If you wish
to discipline the flesh and make it a thousand times more
     subject, then place on it the bridle of love.
Whoever has accepted this sweet burden of the bridle of love
will attain more
and come much further
than all the penitential practices and mortifications
that all the people in the world acting together
could ever carry out.

Whoever has found this way
       needs no other.

It is
      when people are not aware
          of God's presence everywhere

That they must
      seek God by special methods
          and special practices.
      Such people have not attained God.

      To all outward appearances
persons who continue properly in their pious practices
  are holy.
      Inwardly, however,
      they are asses.
For they know about God
but do not know God.

God is like a person who clears his throat while hiding and so gives himself away.

God lies in wait for us with nothing so much as love. Now love is like a fishhook.

A fisher cannot catch a fish unless the fish first picks up the hook. If the fish swallows the hook, no matter how it may squirm and turn the fisher is certain of the fish. Love is the same way. Whoever is captured by love takes up this hook in such a fashion that foot and hand, mouth and eyes, heart and all that is in that person must always belong to God. Therefore, look only for this fishhook, and you will be happily caught. The more you are caught, the more you will be liberated.

As long
     as we perform our works
          in order to go to heaven,
we are simply
     on the wrong track.

     And until
We learn to work
     without a why or wherefore,
     we have not learned to work
     or to live
     or why.

Some people, I swear,
     want to love God in the same way as they love a cow.
     They love it for its milk and cheese and the profit
     they will derive from it.
Those who love God for the sake of outward riches or for
     the sake of inward consolation operate on the
     same principle.
     They are not loving God correctly;
     they are merely loving their own advantage.

One "Hail Mary" uttered sincerely
is more potent
and better
       than a thousand uttered mechanically,
for the heart is not made pure by prayer
but rather
prayer is made pure
          by the pure heart.

When one has learned
to let go
and let be,
then
one is well disposed,
and he or she is always in the right place whether in society
or in solitude.
But if one has a wrong attitude,
    one is always in the wrong place whether in society or not.
Now one who is rightly disposed has God with one
in actual fact in all places, just as much in the street
and in the midst of many people
as in church, or the desert, or a monastic cell.

All paths lead to God
>> For God is on them all evenly
>>> for the person who knows with transformed
>>> knowledge.

What is best
is to take God
>> and enjoy God

in any manner,
>> in any thing,
>>> and not
>> to have to exercise and hunt around
>> for your own special way.

All my life
>> this has been my joy!

PATH III:

BREAKTHROUGH AND BIRTH OF SELF, OF GOD, OF SELF AS SON OR DAUGHTER OF GOD

(Via Creativa)

Our Breakthrough is nobler than our flowing out.
For when I flowed out from God and all creatures
shouted "God!"
they were saying that I was a creature.
And this cannot make me happy.
In my Breakthrough, on the other hand,
I am neither God
nor creature.
Rather,
I am what I was
and what I shall remain now and forever.

In my flowing-out I entered creation,
    In my Breakthrough I re-enter God.

Only those who have dared to let go
    can dare to re-enter.

In this Breakthrough
I discover
      that God and I
            are one.

      There,
      I am what I was,
I grow neither smaller nor bigger,
and I am an immovable cause
that in turn moves all things.

Just as God breaks through me,
so do I break through God in return.

And,
When God draws the soul to him/herself
then the soul becomes divine
but God does not become the soul.

Consider the divine spirit in the human soul.
This spirit is not easily satisfied.
It storms the firmament
and scales the heavens
trying to reach the Spirit that drives the heavens.
Because of this energy
everything in the world grows green,
flourishes,
and bursts into leaf.
But the spirit is never satisfied.
It presses on
deeper and deeper into the vortex
further and further into the whirlpool,
the primary source
in which the spirit has its origin.
This spirit seeks to be
broken through by God.
　　　God leads this spirit
into a desert
into the wilderness and solitude of the divinity
where God is pure unity
and where God gushes up within himself.

I once had a dream.
I dreamt that I, even though a man, was pregnant,
pregnant and full with Nothingness like a woman who
is with child.
And that out of this Nothingness
God was born.

The Word of God
is always 'in the beginning.'
And this means
that it is always in the process of being born
and is always already born.

Now,
it is the nature of a word
to reveal what is hidden.
The Word that is hidden
still sparkles in the darkness
and whispers in the silence.
It entices us to pursue it,
to yearn
              and sigh after it.
For it wishes
to reveal to me
something about God.

Philip once said: "Lord, show us the Father and it is
enough for us."
Do you want the marrow out of which goodness springs?
Do you want the nucleus from which goodness flows?
Do you want the root,
the vein,
from which goodness exudes?
And all beauty?
Then you want the Creator.
And you want your breakthrough.
For remember this:
The shell must be cracked open
if what is inside is to come out.
If you want the kernel,
you must break the shell.
We must learn to break through things
if we are to grasp God in them.

What is my name?
What is your name?
What is God's name?
Our name is:
            that we must be born.
And the Creator's name is:
            to bear.
The soul alone
among all creatures
is generative
like God is.

                    We are all meant
                        to be mothers of God.

Because this Word is a hidden Word
it comes in the darkness of the night.
To enter this darkness put away
all voices and sounds
all images and likenesses.
In stillness and peace
in this unknowing knowledge
God speaks in the soul
and becomes fully expressed there.
For no image has ever reached into the soul's foundation
where God him/herself
with his/her own being
is effective.

In this birth
     you will discover
     all blessing.
But neglect this birth
and you neglect
all blessing.
     Tend only to this birth in you
and you will find there
all goodness and all consolation,
all delight,
all being and all truth.

It is good for a person
to receive God into himself or herself
and I call this receptivity the work of a virgin.
But it is better
when God becomes fruitful within a person.
For becoming fruitful as a result of a gift
is the only gratitude for the gift.
I call such a person a wife
and in this sense the term wife is the noblest term
we can give the soul,
it is far nobler than virgin.
Every day
such a person
bears fruit a hundred times
or a thousand times
or countless times,
giving birth and becoming fruitful
out of the most noble foundation of all.

78

Pay attention now to exactly where this birth takes place:
This eternal birth
takes place in the soul
totally in the manner
in which it takes place in eternity,
neither more nor less.
There is only one birth—
and this birth takes place in the being
and in the ground and core
of the soul.

This birth takes place in darkness.
And not only is the Son of the heavenly Creator
born in this darkness—
but you too
are born there
as a child of the same heavenly Creator
and none other.
And the Creator
extends this same power
to you
out of the divine maternity bed
located in the Godhead
to eternally give birth.

Let me express myself in even a clearer way.
The fruitful person
gives birth
out of the very same foundation
from which the Creator begets the eternal Word
or Creative Energy
and it is from this core
that one becomes fruitfully pregnant.
And in this power of birthing
God is as fully verdant
and as wholly flourishing in full joy
and in all honor
as he/she is in him/herself.
The divine rapture
is unimaginably great.
It is ineffable.

What good is it to me
if this eternal birth of the divine Son
takes place unceasingly
but does not take place
within myself?

    And,
what good is it to me
if Mary is full of grace
and if I am not also full of grace?
What good is it to me
for the Creator to give birth to his/her Son
if I do not also give birth to him
in my time
and my culture?
    This, then,
is the fullness of time:
When the Son of God
is begotten

              in us.

Why is it that some people
do not bear fruit?
It is because they are so busy clinging
to their egotistical attachments
and so afraid of letting go and letting be
that they have no trust
either in God
or in themselves.
Love cannot distrust.
It can only await the good trustfully.
No person
could ever trust God too much.
Nothing people ever do
is as appropriate
as great trust in God.
With such trust,
God never fails to accomplish great things.

What is the test that you have indeed undergone this
holy birth?
Listen carefully.
If this birth has truly taken place within you,
then no creature can any longer hinder you.
Rather, every single creature points you
toward God
and toward this birth.
You receive a rich potential for sensitivity,
a magnificent vulnerability.
In whatever you see or hear, no matter what it is,
you can absorb therein nothing but this birth.
In fact,
everything becomes for you
nothing but God.
For in the midst of all things,
you keep your eye only on God.
To grasp God in all things,
that is the sign
of your new birth.

This is the fullness of time —
when the Son of God
is begotten in you.

Just as you can die of anxiety before a lethal blow is dealt you,
so too can a person
die from an anticipation of joy.
Notice what a wonderful and happy life
a person may have on earth —
a life like God's in heaven.
Here discomfort is like comfort;
grief is like joy.
Eternity is now.

Human beings ought to communicate
and share
all the gifts they have received from God.
If a person has something that
he or she does not share with others,
that person is not good.
A person who does not bestow on others
spiritual things
and the joy that is in them
has in fact never been spiritual.
People are not to receive
and keep gifts for themselves alone,
but should share themselves
and pour forth everything they possess whether in their bodies
or their souls
as much as possible.

The divine countenance
is capable of maddening and driving
all souls out of their senses
with longing for it.
When it does this by its very divine nature
it is thereby
drawing all things to itself.
    Every creature —
whether it knows it or not —
seeks repose.

Whatever
I want to express in its truest meaning
must emerge from within me
and pass through an inner form.
It cannot
come from outside to the inside
but must emerge from within.

Now John says: "Bear fruit that remains." (Jn. 15.16)
But what is it that remains?
It is that which is inborn in me that remains.
The work
that is 'with,' or 'outside' or 'above' the artist
must become the work that is 'in' her,
taking form within her,
in other words
to understand one's vocation as an artist
we should interpret the verse 'The Holy Spirit shall come
      upon thee' (Lk. 1.35) to mean:
'The Holy Spirit shall come from within thee.'

From all eternity
     God lies on a maternity bed
     giving birth.
The essence of God is birthing.

*   *   *   *

Does your heart suffer?
Do the hearts of those around you suffer?
Then,
you are not yet a mother.
You are still on the way to giving birth,
you are only near to birth.

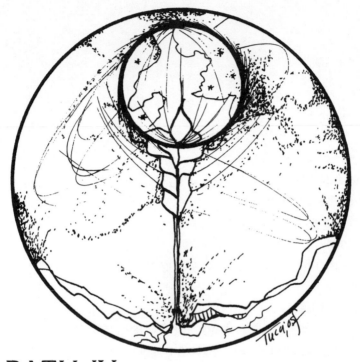

PATH IV:

THE NEW CREATION: COMPASSION AND SOCIAL JUSTICE

(via transformativa)

90

Spirituality
is not to be learned
by flight from the world,
by running away from things,
or by turning solitary and going apart from the world.
Rather,
we must learn an inner solitude
wherever or with whomsoever we may be.
We must learn to penetrate things
and find God there.

The more a person looks on everything as divine—
more divine than it is in itself—
the more will God be pleased.

A person works in a stable.
That person has a Breakthrough.
What does he do?
He returns to work in the stable.

God waits on human history

and suffers as she waits.

*   *   *   *

We ought to get over amusing ourselves with raptures
for the sake of a greater love
which is to minister to what people most need,
whether spiritually
or socially
or physically.

God's ground is my ground
and my ground is God's ground.
Here I live on my own
as God lives on his own.
All our works
should work out of this innermost ground
without a why or a wherefore.
Then,
God and the soul
do one work together
eternally
and very fruitfully.
     Then,
all that this person works
God works.
And just as I can do almost nothing without God,
so too God can accomplish nothing
apart from me.

All virtue of the just
and every work of the just
is nothing other
than the Son—who is the New Creation—
being born from the Father.
In the depths of our being,
where justice and work are one,
we work one work and a New Creation
with God.

People who have let go of themselves are so pure
that the world cannot harm them.
People who love justice
will be admitted to justice,
seized by justice,
and one with justice.
        A just person is one who
is conformed and transformed into justice.
The just person is like God,
for God is justice.
Whoever resides in justice
resides in God
and is God.

God will be born in the just person
just as the just person is born into God.
For the just person,
to act justly is to live;
justice is her life;
her being alive,
her being
to the very extent that she is just.

          In God,
action and being
are one.

People ought to think less about what they should do
and more about what they are.
For when people and their ways are good,
then their works shine forth brightly.
If you are just,
then your works are also just.
Works do not sanctify us—but
we are to sanctify our works.
Holiness is based on being, not on a single action.
If you wish to explore the goodness of actions,
explore first the nature of the ground of the works.

All works are surely dead
if anything from the outside
compels you to work.
Even if it were God himself compelling you to work
from the outside,
your works would be dead.
If your works are to live,
then God must move you from the inside,
from the innermost region of the soul —
then they will really live.
There is your life
and there alone you live
and your works live.

The outward work
will never be puny
if the inward work
is great.
And the outward work
can never be great or even good
if the inward one is puny or of little worth.
The inward work invariably
includes in itself
all expansiveness,
all breadth,
all length,
all depth.
Such a work
receives and draws all its being
from nowhere else except
from and in the heart of God.

Jesus became a human being
because God the compassionate One
could not suffer
and lacked a back to be beaten.
God needed a back like our backs
on which to receive blows
and thereby to perform compassion
as well as to preach it.

How ever great one's suffering is,
if it comes through God,
God suffers from it first.

And remember this:
      All suffering comes to an end.

Compassion
      clothes the soul with the robe of God
          and divinely adorns it.

And those who follow compassion
      find life for themselves,
      justice for their neighbor,
      and glory for God.

Compassion means justice.

    And compassion is just
to the extent that
it gives to each person what is his or hers.

All deeds
      are accomplished in passion.
If the fiery love of God
grows cold in the soul,
the soul dies.
And, in a certain sense,
God dies also.

How can anyone be compassionate toward her neighbor
who is not compassionate toward herself?
This is why Jesus says: "Be compassionate!"
He wants our compassion to begin at home,
he wants us to be compassionate toward our own body
and soul.

Everyone loves himself or herself to some degree.
To do otherwise is to fool yourself.
For if you hated yourself, you would cease to exist.
Since friendly relations with another
spring from friendly relations with yourself,
you should meditate on how it is that
the soul loves the body.
And consider too how it is that
the body is more in the soul
than the soul is in the body.

God has been the common savior
to the entire world.
And this fact delights me
much more
than if God had saved only me.

This is salvation:
When we marvel at the beauty of created things
and praise the beautiful providence of their Creator
or when we purchase heavenly goods
by our compassion
for the works of creation.

By compassion
the soul is made blessed.

When Moses descended from the mountain
and came announcing a land flowing with milk and honey
that milk and honey
was humanity and divinity.
Compassion flows when humanity and divinity flow.

In compassion
justice and peace kiss.
We have to run into peace,
we do not begin in peace.
What is born of God
seeks peace
and runs into peace.
The person who runs and runs,
continually running toward peace,
is a heavenly person.
Even the heavens
are continually running
and in their running
are seeking peace.

The fullest work
that God ever worked
in any creature
is compassion.
The most secret and forbidden work
that God ever worked on the angels
was carrying them into compassion.
This is the work of compassion
as it is in itself
and as it is in God.
Whatever God does,
the first outburst is always compassion.
I do not mean that God forgives a person his sins
or that a person takes pity on another.
I mean much more.
I mean that the highest work that God ever works is
compassion.

The highest work of God is compassion.
　　And this means that God sets the soul
in the highest and purest place which it can occupy:
in space,
in the sea,
in a fathomless ocean,
and there
God works compassion.
This is why the prophet writes: "Lord, have compassion
on the people who are in you." (Ho. 14.4)
What people are in God?
John says: "God is love and
whoever remains in love
remains in God
and God in her." (1 Jn. 4.16)

You may call God love
you may call God goodness.
But the best name for God is

                              compassion.

You ask me what the human soul is?
No human science can ever fathom what the soul is in
its depth.
What the soul is in its ground,
no one knows.
But this we do know:
That the soul is
      where God works compassion.

God's peace
prompts service among brothers and sisters.
In that way one creature
sustains another.
One enriches the other,
and that is why
all creatures are interdependent.

All are sent
or no one is sent,
into all
or into nothing.
For in the kingdom of heaven,
all is in all,
all is one
and all is ours.
                    And,

In the kingdom of heaven
everything
is in everything else.
All is one
and all is ours.

We are all in all
as God
is all in all.

To live the wayless way
free and yet bound
learn to live
among things but not *in* things.
All God's friends live this way—
among cares
but not within cares.
How wonderful it is to be so spiritually mature
that one exists
both outside and inside,
one seizes and is seized,
one sees and is seen,
one holds and is held—
that is the goal where the spirit remains at rest
united to eternity.
There our work and activity in time
are just as noble and as full of joy
as Mary Magdelene's retreat in the desert.
Remember Martha who in her spiritual maturity
was so real
that her works did not hinder her.

We are fellow-helpers with God,
co-creators in everything we do.
When Word and work are returned to their source
and origin
then all work is accomplished divinely in God.
And there too
the soul loses itself
in a wonderful enchantment.

God wills all persons to be saved.
Pray for the whole world,
bid this very earth to become a heaven.
Pray especially
to be freed from the evil of greediness.
Pray to recognize others who are in need—
for there is no such thing as "my" bread.
All bread is *ours*
and is given to me,
to others through me
and to me through others.
For not only bread
but all things necessary for sustenance in this life
are given on loan to us
with others
and because of others,
and for others
and to others through us.

Whoever
does not give to another
what belongs to that other
does not eat his own bread
but steals the bread of that other.
For nothing
that we have acquired unjustly
is ours.

All gifts of nature and of grace
have been given us on loan.
Their ownership is not ours, but God's.
God never gave personal property to anyone—
not even to his Mother
or to any other person
or to any creature in any way.
Treat all things as if they were loaned to you
without any ownership—
whether body or soul,
sense or strength,
external goods or honors,
friends or relations,
house or hall,
everything.
For if I want to possess the property I have
instead of receive it on loan,
then I want to be a master.

I have told you this time and time again.
If a person
were in a rapture
as great as St. Paul once experienced
and learned that her neighbor were in need of a cup of soup,
it would be best
to withdraw from the rapture
and give the person
the soup she needs.

The poor
are all too often
left to God.
Therefore,
forget those who are better placed
and remember the poor.

Humanity in the poorest and most despised human being
is just as complete
as in the Pope
or the Emperor.
Also,
humanity is dearer to me
than the human being
I carry about in myself.

What do the poor do
who endure illness and suffering
that is equal to or greater than your own
and have no one to give them
so much as a glass of cold water?
They must seek their dry bread
come rain, cold or snow
from house to house.
Therefore, if you want to be comforted
comfort those worse off than yourself
and there are many.

Being a rich man
      does not make one wise.

I will tell you a peculiar thing about myself:
I much prefer a person who loves God enough
to take a handout of bread
to him who gives the handout in the first place.
Why?
Because the giver buys his honor;
but the beggar sells his.

Love
will never be anywhere
except where equality and unity are.
Between a master and his servant
there is no peace
for there is no real equality.
And there can be no love
where love does not find equality
or is not busy creating equality.
Nor is there any pleasure
without equality.
Practice equality in human society.
Learn to love, esteem, consider all people
like yourself.
What happens to another,
be it bad or good, pain or joy,
ought to be as if it happened to you.

Every human person is an aristocrat,
every human person is noble and of royal blood.
Who is more noble than someone who is born,
on the one hand,
from the highest and best that a creature possesses
and who, on the other hand,
is born
from the intimate depths of the divine nature
and the divine wilderness?

When people grow and become rooted in love and in God,
they are ready to take upon themselves
every attack,
temptation,
vexation,
and painful suffering willingly and gladly,
eagerly and joyfully
like the prophets.
You flee from care and throw off fear
when you more and more forsake your mothers
and depart farther and farther from the womb.
And do not be afraid to cut yourself off from your fathers.
People should not feel bad if others are angry with them
but only if they merited the anger.

What is the mark of a good person?
    A good person
        praises good people.

A royal person
derives
and creates
his or her whole being, life and happiness
only from God, through God and in God.
To find God
you must become one.
Be one,
so that you can find God!
Be
        one with one,
        one from one,
        one in one,
        and externally one in one.

Do you want to know
what goes on in the core of the Trinity?
I will tell you.
In the core of the Trinity
the Father laughs
and gives birth to the Son.
The Son laughs back at the Father
and gives birth to the Spirit.
The whole Trinity laughs
and gives birth to us.

All things love God.

At every deed, however puny,
that results in justice,
God is made glad,
glad through and through.
At such a time
there is nothing in the core of the Godhead
that is not tickled through and through
and that does not dance for joy.

The path of which I have spoken
    is beautiful
        and pleasant
            and joyful
                and familiar.

Let whoever has found this way
    seek no other
    and you shall find
    that God
        who is whole and entire
        will possess you whole and entire.

BOOKS OF RELATED INTEREST

Passion for Creation
The Earth-Honoring Spirituality of Meister Eckhart
by Matthew Fox

A Spirituality Named Compassion
Uniting Mystical Awareness with Social Justice
by Matthew Fox

A New Reformation
Creation Spirituality and the Transformation of Christianity
by Matthew Fox

Illuminations of Hildegard of Bingen
by Matthew Fox

Hildegard of Bingen's Book of Divine Works
With Letters and Songs
Edited by Matthew Fox

Meditations with Hildegard of Bingen
Edited by Gabriele Uhlein

Meditations with Teilhard de Chardin
Edited by Blanche Gallagher

Meditations with Julian of Norwich
Edited by Brendan Doyle

Inner Traditions • Bear & Company
P.O. Box 388
Rochester, VT 05767
1-800-246-8648
www.InnerTraditions.com

Or contact your local bookseller